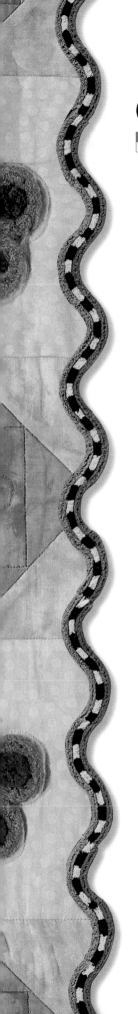

W9-DGE-950

the
Thrill of Chenille

Fran Morgan

American Quilter's Society

P. O. Box 3290 • Paducah, KY 42002-3290
www.AQSquilt.com

The Thrill of Chenille

Located in Paducah, Kentucky, the American Quilter's Society (AQS) is dedicated to promoting the accomplishments of today's quilters. Through its publications and events, AQS strives to honor today's quiltmakers and their work and to inspire future creativity and innovation in quiltmaking.

EDITOR: SHELLEY HAWKINS
GRAPHIC DESIGN: AMY CHASE
COVER DESIGN: MICHAEL BUCKINGHAM
QUILT PHOTOGRAPHY: CHARLES R. LYNCH (unless otherwise noted)

Library of Congress Cataloging-in-Publication Data

Morgan, Fran.
  Fabric café : the thrill of chenille / by Fran Morgan.
    p. cm.
  ISBN 1-57432-847-6
 1, Quilting--Patterns. 2. Chenille. I. Title.

    TT835.M6789 2004
    746.46--dc22

                 2004001017

Additional copies of this book may be ordered from the American Quilter's Society, PO Box 3290, Paducah, KY 42002-3290, or online at www.AQSquilt.com.

Copyright © 2004, Fran Morgan

All rights reserved. No part of this book may be reproduced, stored in any retrieval system, or transmitted in any form, or by any means including but not limited to electronic, mechanical, photocopy, recording, or otherwise, without the written consent of the author and publisher. Patterns may be copied for personal use only.

No work is ever accomplished alone. I want to say a special thank you to Jessica Greene, who was so instrumental in assisting me with every stage of quiltmaking. She enthusiastically assisted in color selection, art preparation, and quilt assembly. Her creative ideas connected so well with mine that we often became giddy with excitement as we fleshed out an idea.

Others supporting me in this endeavor were my husband, Mel Morgan, and my son, Blake, who exercised endless patience for my quilting while the dust bunnies drifted across the floor and lodged in the fast-food containers left from dinner.

Also, thanks are in order for Cindy Landrum, Denise Thelman, friends and co-workers, and Blake Rohus, who willingly helped with materials preparation for the quilts.

Thanks to Donna Robertson, my business partner and mother, who believes in me and my talents and supports me as I reach for the stars. Together, we work tirelessly through the development and marketing of Fabric Café® products and share in the joy of seeing a dream come alive.

Contents

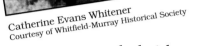

Catherine Evans Whitener
Courtesy of Whitfield-Murray Historical Society

Sometimes I sit in my quilting studio and wonder how my chosen career affects those around me. To some, my job doesn't seem all that important on a vast, worldly scale. You see, I quilt. I play in my studio and design bright, colorful quilts embellished with chenille textures. However, the story of Catherine Evans Whitener, who is credited with founding the chenille bedspread industry, helps me get a new perspective.

In 1892, 12-year-old Catherine visited her cousin in McCurthey, Georgia. During that visit, Catherine was shown a tufted bedspread, which was a treasured family heirloom. The technique for making the spread was considered out-of-date, but it made an impression on young Catherine, sparking a desire to replicate the heirloom.

By the age of 15, Catherine produced a spread that she gave as a gift to her sister-in-law. Others saw the spread and Catherine soon found herself busily reproducing the spreads by special request. To fill these requests, she developed a series of steps to make her job easier.

First, Catherine sewed flour sacks together to make a large piece of cloth. She placed the cloth on top of a finished spread and rubbed a baking tin smeared with soot over the blank cloth. This transferred the design of the bumps from the finished spread. Next, she stitched small loops with a thick yarn created from 12 twisted strands of cotton twine. Once stitched, the brightly colored yarn loops were clipped, creating what resembled short fringe. She then boiled the spread several times to remove soot left from the transfer process and shrank the flour sack material to hold the tufts tightly in place.

Finally, the spreads were hung on clotheslines to be beaten and brushed, which separated the fibers of cotton yarn to create full, fluffy chenille. The demand for Catherine's beautiful spreads became intense among family and friends, so she began teaching others the tedious techniques she had developed.

Eventually, others recognized the value of Catherine's creations and identified an opportunity to gain their fortunes. With the help of fresh capital backing this business venture, and partnerships with those who created tufting machines, factories were built and business thrived. Catherine's hometown of Dalton, Georgia, became known as the home of the bedspread industry. At the height of the chenille craze, more than 10,000 workers were employed and sales yielded over $25 million annually.

Many lives were affected by those early creative endeavors of a 12-year-old girl. In pondering my chosen career, I think of you holding this book. As you peruse the pages, I hope you find inspiration, and with each quilt you make, realize that your creative endeavors are like one thread in a universal cloth of creativity, touching the lives of many unknown persons. Happy quilting!

Basic Instructions

Overview

- Use a ¼" seam allowance on all projects, unless otherwise stated.

- Prewash all fabrics, but never prewash Chenille By The Inch™.

- Cut all pieces listed in the materials box before beginning the project. The following is a cutting key for symbols in the list:

    ◻ cut once diagonally
    ⊠ cut twice diagonally

- To ensure that the seam allowance is not brushed out, never brush Chenille By The Inch until the project is complete.

- When using dark colors of chenille on a light background, use very little water during the brushing process to avoid bleeding. When laundering, use a product that absorbs loose dye particles. This product is available where laundry supplies are sold.

Supplies

For successful quilt projects, good supplies are a necessity. There are several basic supplies that are needed when working with Chenille By The Inch. The following is a brief description of these supplies and how they are used.

Rotary Cutter

A rotary cutter has proven to be an invaluable tool when cutting quilt pieces. It is also wonderful when cutting strips of chenille. The rotary cutter will cut a clean, precise strip.

Chenille Cutting Guide™

The stitched lines on Chenille By The Inch are ⅜" apart. To cut in the center between these stitched lines, you need to measure 3⁄16" from each line. The Chenille Cutting Guide is marked to make perfectly cut strips simple. Just place the line of the guide on top of a stitched line, then cut through all thicknesses of fabric with a rotary cutter.

Chenille Brush™

The Chenille Brush is the perfect tool for separating the fibers of chenille all the way to the stitching line and creating the fluffiest chenille. The nylon bristle is very stiff, so it separates the fibers quickly without damaging most basic quilting cotton background fabrics. For the fastest results when brushing, keep the brush flat on the surface, allowing all the bristles to work for you.

Spray Bottle

During the brushing process, spraying the chenille strips lightly with distilled water softens the sizing in the fabric and speeds the fluffing process. It's important to use distilled water because tap water may include chlorine, which acts as a bleaching agent and could cause color damage.

Fabric Marker

Fabric markers are used to transfer chenille and embroidery lines to your projects. There are many different types of fabric-marking tools available, including water-soluble, disappearing, iron-on transfer, and chalk. Always test the marker on a scrap of fabric to see if the one you've chosen produces a clear, distinct line.

Scissors

Keep a sharp pair of scissors in your work station for trimming threads and the ends of chenille strips.

Stiletto or Fabric Tool

A fabric tool such as a stiletto or Trolley Needle™ helps when sewing chenille in tight curves. It enables you to adjust your work directly under the presser foot without getting your fingers near the needle.

Chenille Packs from Fabric Café®. See page 80.

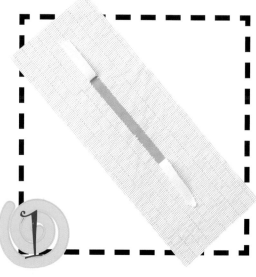

Chenille By The Inch

1 Hold Chenille By The Inch in the center and pull to remove the tear-away backing. The backing will begin to separate at the stitching lines and easily pull away. For quick removal of the backing and to keep the stitches secure, remove every other channel of the backing, pulling from the center to the edges.

Note: The tear-away backing on Chenille By The Inch is extremely heat sensitive and should not be placed near irons or other heat-producing items.

2 With a rotary cutter and Chenille Cutting Guide, cut the chenille into strips. Place the line of the guide directly on top of the second stitching line from one edge. Holding the guide securely, cut the chenille into ⅜" wide strips. The strips should have an equal amount of fabric on either side of the stitched line.

3 Using your preferred fabric marking method and referring to the project patterns, transfer the chenille placement lines to the background fabric.

Sew the chenille strips to the background by aligning the center stitching line of the strip with the transferred pattern line. Do not cut the length of the strips until they are sewn in place. Chenille By The Inch can be sewn directly to the background fabric without pinning or basting. Because chenille is sewn on the bias, avoid stretching the strips as you sew them in place.

You can use every inch of Chenille By The Inch. Create continuous lines of chenille as you complete each strip by overlapping the strip ¼" with the end of a new strip, back-stitch, and continue sewing. Always back-stitch to secure a new strip thoroughly. Pause with your needle in the down position to keep from pulling the strip off center.

4 Brushing is an essential part of creating full, fluffy chenille. Once the project is completely sewn with no raw edges exposed, give a section of the sewn strips a quick overall brushing to roughen the edges. Next, lightly spray that section with distilled water. Brush again. Once the piece is brushed and dried, the chenille will be full and fluffy. For maximum bloom, launder the finished project to wash out all the sizing.

Note: When working with background fabrics that may be sensitive to brushing, such as flannels, knits, and textured fabrics, transfer the appliqué pattern and chenille placement lines to a tear-away stabilizer. Matching the appliquéd pattern, pin the stabilizer to the background fabric. Sew the chenille on top of the stabilizer and background fabric. Brush the chenille before removing the stabilizer.

Step-by-step photos courtesy of Fabric Café®

Materials

⅓ yard natural-fiber fabric
Tear-away stabilizer
Temporary spray adhesive
Fabric marker
Straight pins
Quilting guide for your sewing machine
Sewing thread to match fabric

Making Your Own Chenille Strips

With Chenille By the Inch, you can skip the time-consuming steps of layering and stitching the fabrics for chenille strips and go straight to the creative aspect of the process. However, there may be an occasion when you'll want to make your own chenille strips. These easy-to-follow steps will help you.

Choose a natural-fiber fabric such as cotton, linen, silk, or rayon. Chenille By The Inch is made with 100 percent cotton. Different fabrics will "chenille" differently, so it is important to test a swatch before purchasing a large quantity of fabric. It is also best that you don't prewash the fabric. The extra sizing left in the fabric helps stabilize it as the layers are sewn together.

You will need three layers of fabric, plus a layer of tear-away stabilizer. I prefer making chenille strips in 12" squares. It's an easy size to handle while sewing and makes approximately 325 linear inches of chenille strips.

1 Cut three 12" squares of fabric on the straight of grain and one 12" square of tear-away stabilizer. Spray the stabilizer with temporary adhesive and place one piece of fabric on top of the stabilizer, matching edges. Spray the remaining two pieces of fabric with temporary adhesive and, matching edges, place on top of the fabric and stabilizer package. With a fabric marker, draw a line diagonally through opposite corners of the fabric.

2 With matching thread and 10 stitches per inch or smaller, sew through all thicknesses following the marked line. The stitched line must be on the bias. With a quilting guide, continue sewing lines ⅜" from the first sewn line. If the layers of fabric begin to slip, pin to secure. Continue sewing until the lines cover the entire fabric. *Note: The sample was made with contrasting thread for photo purposes.*

 Remove the tear-away stabilizer, pulling it from the center to the outside edges of the square.

 With a straight edge and rotary cutter, cut the chenille into strips ³⁄₁₆" from the stitched lines.

Appliqué

Before using paper-backed fusible web, refer to the manufacturer's instructions for fabric preparation, heat settings, and usage.

1. Trace the project patterns to the paper side of the fusible web. Cut the patterns apart, leaving a small margin beyond the drawn lines.

2. Adhere the traced patterns to the wrong side of the appropriate fabrics. The fabric and cutting list for the projects indicates which fabric should be used for each pattern piece. Cut the patterns apart following the traced lines.

3. Peel the paper from the cut-out piece. With the wrong (shiny) side to the background fabric, adhere.

4. Finish the edges of the pattern pieces as stated in the project. Most pieces require a blanket or satin stitch. A French knot is used in the CAT AND MOUSE QUILT.

Projects

Bebop Quilt

Finished size: 61" x 84"

Fabric and Cutting

WOF means width of fabric.
Yardage is based on a 40"–45" WOF.

Fabric	Yards	Cut	Dimension
Purple	1¾	66	5½" squares
Blue	2¾		
border		8	1½" x WOF
binding		8	2¼" x WOF
blocks		66	5½" squares
Green	1¼		
border		8	1½" x WOF
blocks		33	5½" squares
Black	⅓	6	1½" x WOF
White	⅓	6	1½" x WOF
Backing	5	2	85" x WOF

Chenille By The Inch

Color		Amount
12	Coconut	180"
14	Licorice	180"
07	Limeade	325"
09	Blue Moon	325"

Additional Materials

Additional Materials
Basic supplies as listed, pages 6 and 7
Blue sewing thread
Full-sized (81" x 96") cotton batting
Light purple quilting thread

1 *Note: Correct placement of chenille on the blocks is essential for the successful flow of colors on the assembled quilt.* With a fabric marker, transfer the chenille placement lines, page 15, to the purple blocks. Referring to Chenille By The Inch instructions, page 8, prepare the chenille strips for sewing.

Cut the Licorice and Coconut chenille into 1" pieces. Following the chenille color guide and starting at the center edge of the purple blocks, sew the chenille in place, overlapping the ends of each piece ⅛". Add the remaining strips of chenille to the blocks. Make 33 A blocks and 33 B blocks.

2 Referring to the quilt assembly guide, page 16, sew the purple, blue, and green blocks together in 15 strips of 11 blocks. Sew the strips together.

3 Sew the ends of two 1½" green strips together and press the seam allowances open. Repeat for the remaining green strips. Sew the pieced strips to the sides, then to the top and bottom of the quilt top. Press and trim each strip to size.

4 Referring to the border assembly guide, page 14, sew three black and three white 1½" strips together. Make two strip-sets. Cut the sets into 1½" segments. Make 46 segments. For each long side of the quilt, sew the ends of 13 segments together. For the top and bottom of the quilt, sew the ends of 10 segments together. Sew the pieced segments to the sides, then to the top and bottom of the quilt top. Press and trim each strip to size.

5 Sew the ends of two 1½" blue strips together and press the seam allowances open. Repeat for the remaining blue strips. Sew the pieced strips to the sides, then to the top and bottom of the quilt top. Press and trim each strip to size.

6 Sew the backing pieces together along the 85" length and press the seam allowance open. Layer and baste the quilt top, batting, and backing. Machine quilt as desired (see suggestion, page 16). Sew the binding to the quilt, mitering corners. Fold the binding to the back, press, and hand stitch.

7 Referring to Chenille By The Inch instructions, page 9, use a spray bottle with distilled water to lightly mist the sewn chenille strips. Brush vigorously to fluff the chenille.

Continuous-Line Quilting Pattern

Border Assembly

1½"   1½"   1½"

Bebop Quilt
Chenille Color Guide

Blocks A and B
Make 33 of each

12	Coconut
14	Licorice
07	Limeade
09	Blue Moon

block center

¼" seam allowance*

*To eliminate bulk in seams,
begin and end the chenille
¼" away from the block edge.

block center

Block A

Block B

Quilting Suggestion

The BEBOP QUILT was triple echo quilted around the wavy lines of chenille. The continuous-line daisy pattern, page 14, was quilted in the center of the green blocks. The remaining areas between the chenille and the green blocks were stipple quilted.

Quilt Assembly

Cat and Mouse Quilt

Finished size: 60" x 60"

Fabric and Cutting

WOF means width of fabric.
Yardage is based on a 40"–45" WOF. An "r"
indicates that a pattern should be reversed.

Fabric	Yards	Cut	Dimension
Blue print	1⅝		
binding		7	2¼ x WOF
cat blocks		9	12½" squares
Yellow print	½		
mouse blocks		8	6½" squares
Gold	1		
cat face		9	A, page 20
cat body		9	B, page 21
mouse tummy		8	F, page 22
mouse ears		16	G, page 22
Red	2¼		
sashing		12	6½" x 12½"
border		8	6½" x 24½"
cat stripes		9 each	C, Cr, D & Dr, page 21
Blue	¼		
mouse body		8	E, page 22
Backing	3¾	2	64" x WOF

Chenille By The Inch

Color	Amount
01 Strawberry	350"

Additional Materials
Basic supplies as listed, pages 6 and 7
Paper-backed fusible web
Red sewing thread
Gold, black, and blue embroidery thread
Black and red embroidery floss
Twin-sized (72" x 90") cotton batting
Monofilament quilting thread
18 blue ½" buttons for cat eyes

1 Referring to Appliqué instructions, page 11, transfer patterns A through G to the paper side of the fusible web and fuse them to the wrong side of the appropriate fabrics. Cut the patterns out on the drawn line. Fuse B to the center edge of the 12½" blue squares, then fuse A, C, Cr, D, and Dr to B. Fuse E to the center of the 6½" yellow squares, then fuse F and G to E.

2 With gold embroidery thread, appliqué the edges of the cat face and body with a blanket stitch. With a fabric marker, transfer the embroidery and chenille placement lines to the cats and mice. With black embroidery thread and a standard stitch width, satin stitch the cat mouth and paw lines. Decreasing the stitch width by half, satin stitch the whisker and claw lines.

With blue thread and a standard stitch width, satin stitch the mouse tail and edges of E. With gold thread, satin stitch the edges of G. With black thread and decreasing the stitch width by half, satin stitch the whisker and mouth lines. Embroider the mouse eyes with black floss in French knots. Embroider the mouse nose with red floss in French knots.

3 Referring to Chenille By The Inch instructions, page 8, prepare the chenille strips for sewing. To make the cat nose, cut a ⅜" piece from the chenille strip and sew it to the placement line on A. Sew chenille to the edges of the cat stripes and ears and the mouse tummies.

4 Referring to the quilt assembly guide, page 23, piece the center of the quilt top in five strips of cat and mouse blocks and sashing. Sew the strips together.

5 Sew two 6½" x 24½" red strips together along the short ends and press the seam allowances open. Repeat with the remaining red strips. Sew a pieced strip to each side of the quilt top and press. Sew one mouse block to each end of the remaining strips, then sew the strips to the top and bottom of the quilt top.

6 Sew the backing pieces together along the 64" length and press the seam allowance open. Layer and baste the quilt top, batting, and backing. Machine quilt as desired (see suggestion, page 23). Sew the binding to the quilt, mitering corners. Fold the binding to the back, press, and hand stitch.

7 Referring to Chenille By The Inch instructions, page 9, use a spray bottle with distilled water to lightly mist the sewn chenille strips. Brush vigorously to fluff the chenille.

8 For cat eyes, sew the buttons to A, following the placement dots. *Note: Quilts with buttons should not be given to children under the age of five. Substitute small appliqué circles for the eyes if the quilt is for small children.*

The chenille required for this project has been designed especially for the American Quilter's Society by Fabric Café®. See page 80.

Cat and Mouse Quilt
Chenille Color & Stitch Guide

01	Strawberry	————————
MWW	Satin Stitch	————————
mmmm	Half-Wide Satin Stitch	————————

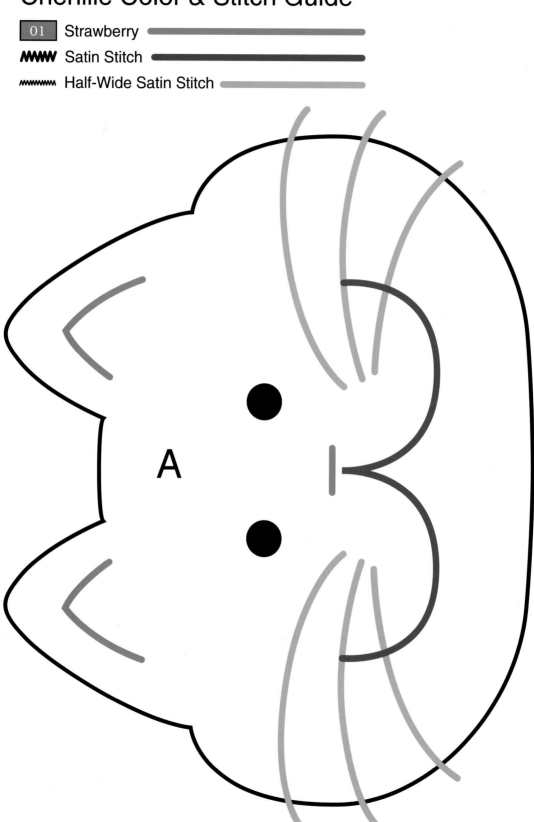

Cat and Mouse Quilt
Chenille Color & Stitch Guide

| 01 | Strawberry |
| Satin Stitch |
| Half-Wide Satin Stitch |

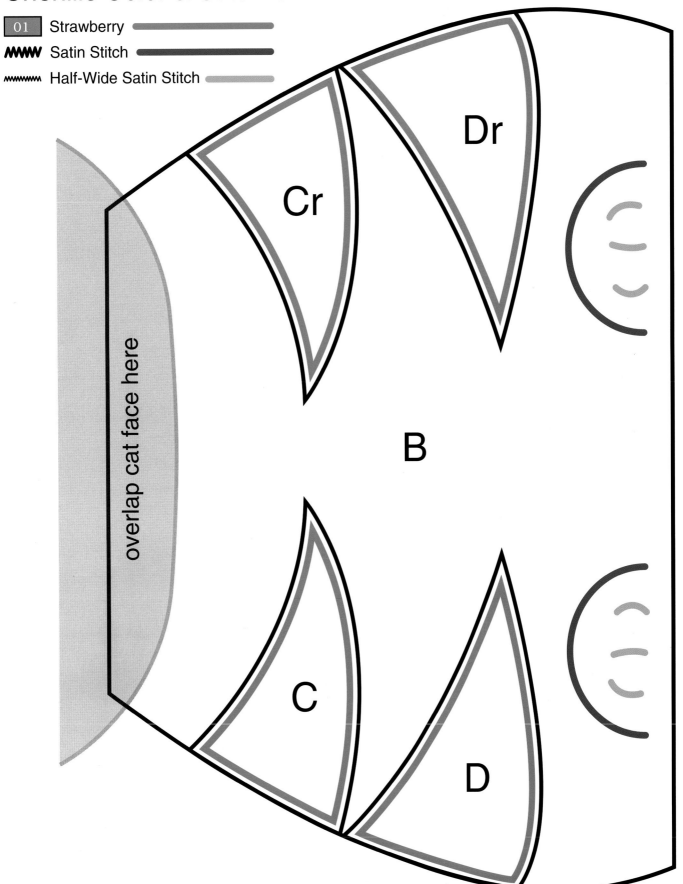

overlap cat face here

Cr

Dr

B

C

D

Cat and Mouse Quilt
Chenille Color & Stitch Guide

01	Strawberry	
MMMW	Satin Stitch	
mmmmm	Half-Wide Satin Stitch	

Quilting Suggestion

The CAT AND MOUSE QUILT was free-motion stipple quilted.

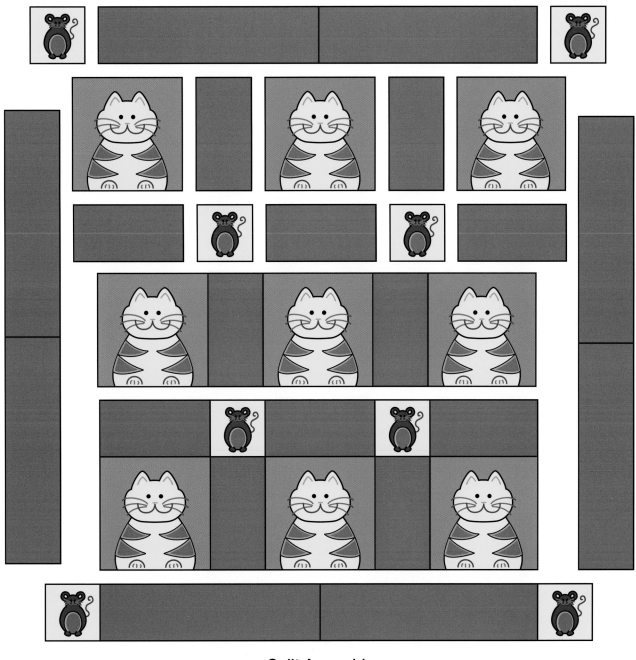

Quilt Assembly

Golden Treasures Quilt

Finished size: 58½" x 79½"

Fabric and Cutting

WOF means width of fabric.
Yardage is based on a 40"–45" WOF.

Fabric	Yards	Cut	Dimension
Gold	3		
border		8	1½" x WOF
background blocks		17	11" squares
Star blocks		12	4¾" squares, cut ⊠
Shoo Fly blocks		12	4⅜" squares, cut ◻
Diamond blocks		24	3½" squares, cut ◻
Red	2½		
border		8	1½" x WOF
binding		8	2¼" x WOF
Star blocks		24	4" squares
		12	4¾" squares, cut ⊠
Shoo Fly blocks		24	4" squares
		12	4⅜" squares, cut ◻
Diamond blocks		24	2⅝" squares
		24	3½" squares, cut ◻
Multi-colored print	1⅜		
border		8	1½" x WOF
Star blocks		6	4" squares
Shoo Fly blocks		6	4" squares
Diamond blocks		24	3½" squares, cut ◻
large flower buds		6	A, page 27
small flower buds		56	B, page 27
Backing	4½	2	80" x WOF

Chenille By The Inch

Color		Amount
17	Basil	830"
16	Wine	240"
15	Chocolate	30"

Additional Materials
Basic supplies as listed, pages 6 and 7
Gold sewing thread
Paper-backed fusible web
Twin-sized (72" x 90") cotton batting
Monofilament quilting thread

1 Referring to the block assembly guides, page 28, piece a Star block with eight gold triangles, eight red triangles, four red squares, and one multi-colored square. Make six Star blocks.

Piece a Shoo Fly block as shown with four gold triangles, four red triangles, four red squares, and one multi-colored square. Make six Shoo Fly blocks.

Piece a Diamond block as shown with eight gold triangles, eight red triangles, eight multi-colored triangles, and four red squares. Make six Diamond blocks.

2 Fold each 11" gold block in half, then in half again, and finger press to mark the center. With a fabric marker, transfer flower patterns 1, 2, and 3 and the chenille placement lines to the center of the blocks. Make six blocks of patterns 1 and 2 and five blocks of pattern 3.

3 Referring to Appliqué instructions, page 11, transfer A and B to the paper side of the fusible web and fuse them to the wrong side of the appropriate fabrics. Cut the patterns out on the drawn line. Fuse A and B to the blocks, following the transferred placement lines. With red embroidery thread, appliqué the edges of the patterns with a blanket stitch.

Referring to Chenille By The Inch instructions, page 8, prepare the chenille strips and sew them to the blocks.

5 Piece the center section of the quilt top in seven strips of five blocks as shown in the quilt assembly guide, page 29. Sew the strips together.

6 Sew two 1½" multi-colored strips together along the short ends and press the seam allowances open. Repeat with the remaining multi-colored strips. Sew the pieced strips to the top and bottom, then to the sides of the quilt top. Press and trim each strip to size.

Sew the 1½" gold strips together in pairs and the 1½" red strips together in pairs, then sew the pieced strips to the quilt top in the same manner.

7 Sew the backing pieces together along the 80" length and press the seam allowance open. Layer and baste the quilt top, batting, and backing. Machine quilt as desired (see suggestion, page 29). Sew the binding to the quilt, mitering corners. Fold the binding to the back, press, and hand stitch.

8 Referring to Chenille By The Inch instructions, page 9, use a spray bottle with distilled water to lightly mist the sewn chenille strips. Brush vigorously to fluff the chenille.

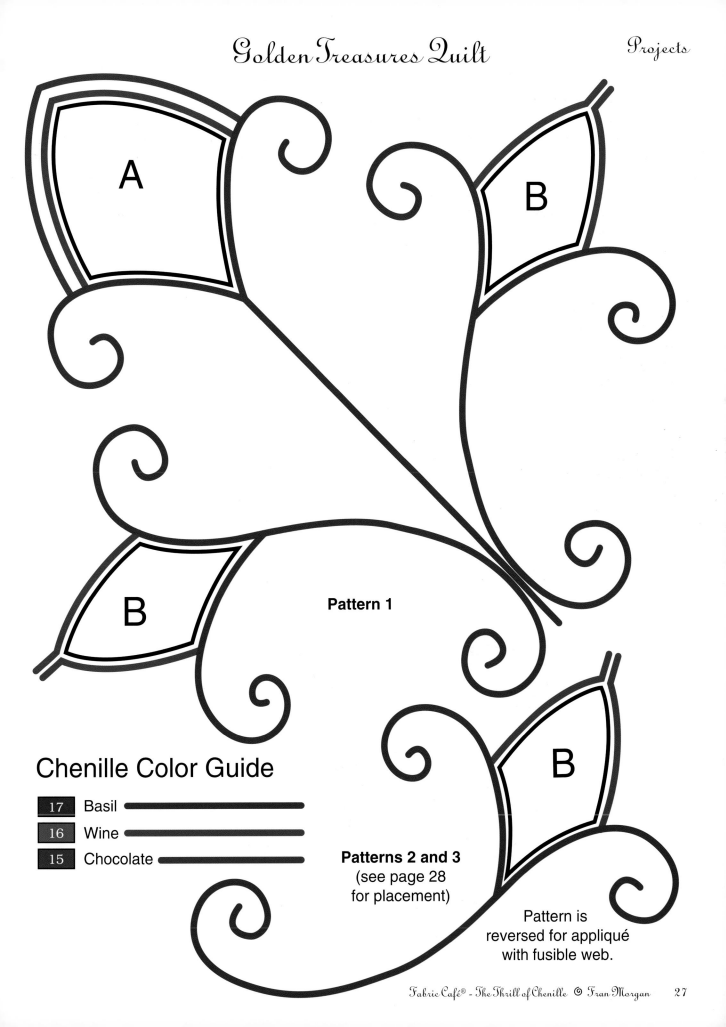

Golden Treasures Quilt

A

B

B

Pattern 1

B

Chenille Color Guide

17	Basil
16	Wine
15	Chocolate

Patterns 2 and 3
(see page 28
for placement)

Pattern is
reversed for appliqué
with fusible web.

Golden Treasures Quilt

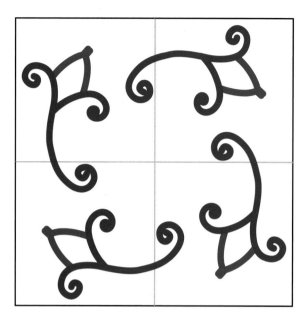

Pattern 2
Placement Guide

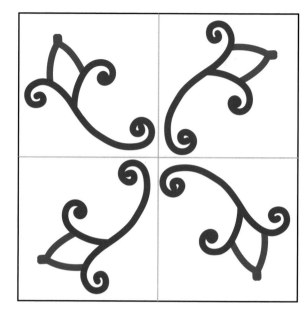

Pattern 3
Placement Guide

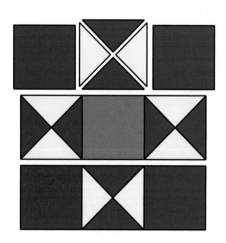

Star Block Assembly

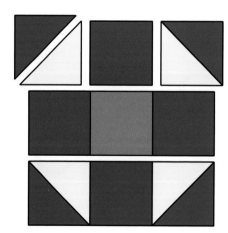

Shoo Fly Block Assembly

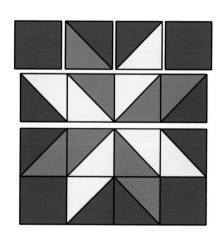

Diamond Block Assembly

Quilting Suggestion

The GOLDEN TREASURES QUILT was quilted in the ditch, then the flower blocks were free-motion echo quilted. The pieced blocks were quilted ¼" inside the seams and with a triple-line design in some areas. The border strips were quilted with a line through the center.

Quilt Assembly

Just Plane Fun Quilt

Finished size: 38" x 46"

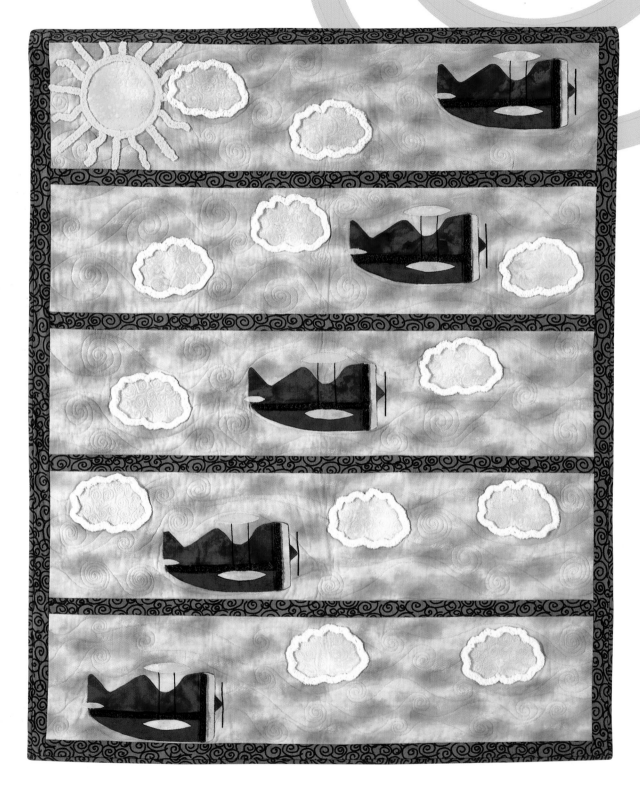

Fabric and Cutting

WOF means width of fabric.
Yardage is based on a 40"–45" WOF.

Fabric	Yards	Cut	Dimension
Blue	1¼		
background		5	8½" x 36½"
Green	1		
sashing and border		10	1½" x WOF
binding		5	2¼" x WOF
Light blue	¼		
clouds		12	A, page 33
Red	⅜		
airplane body		5	B, page 34
Royal blue	¼		
airplane bottom		5	C, page 34
Yellow	¼		
airplane wings		5	D, page 34
airplane tail wings		5	E, page 34
airplane noses		5	F, page 34
sun		1	G, page 35
Backing	1½	1	50" x WOF

Chenille By The Inch

	Color	Amount
12	Coconut	175"
02	Parsley	60"
08	Banana	50"

Additional Materials

Basic supplies as listed, pages 6 and 7
Paper-backed fusible web
White sewing thread
Red, yellow, blue, and black embroidery thread
Crib-sized (45" x 60") cotton batting
Monofilament quilting thread

(1) Referring to Appliqué instructions, page 11, transfer patterns A through G to the paper side of the fusible web and fuse them to wrong side of the appropriate fabrics. Cut the patterns out on the drawn line.

Following the quilt assembly guide, page 36, and placement lines on B, fuse the airplanes, clouds, and sun to the 8½" x 36½" blue backgrounds. *Note: When fusing pieces, leave ¼" for the seam allowance on all sides of the background.* With a blanket stitch and matching embroidery thread for each piece, appliqué the edges of B through F.

(2) With a fabric marker, transfer the embroidery and chenille placement lines to the airplanes, clouds, and sun. With black embroidery thread, satin stitch the wing and propeller lines.

(3) Referring to Chenille By The Inch instructions, page 8, prepare the chenille strips and sew them to the airplanes, clouds, and sun.

The chenille required for this project has been designed especially for the American Quilter's Society by Fabric Café®. See page 80.

4 Following the quilt assembly guide, sew sashing and background pieces together. Press and trim the ends of the sashing to size. Sew two 1½" strips together along the short end and press the seam allowance open. Repeat with the remaining two strips. Sew one pieced strip to each side of the quilt top. Press and trim each strip to size.

5 Layer and baste the quilt top, batting, and backing. Machine quilt as desired (see suggestion, page 36). Sew the binding to the quilt, mitering corners. Fold the binding to the back, press, and hand stitch.

6 Referring to Chenille By The Inch instructions, page 9, use a spray bottle with distilled water to lightly mist the sewn chenille strips. Brush vigorously to fluff the chenille.

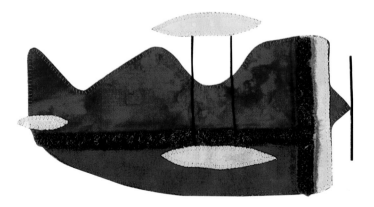

Just Plane Fun Quilt

Chenille Color Guide

| 12 | Coconut ⊂══════════════⊃

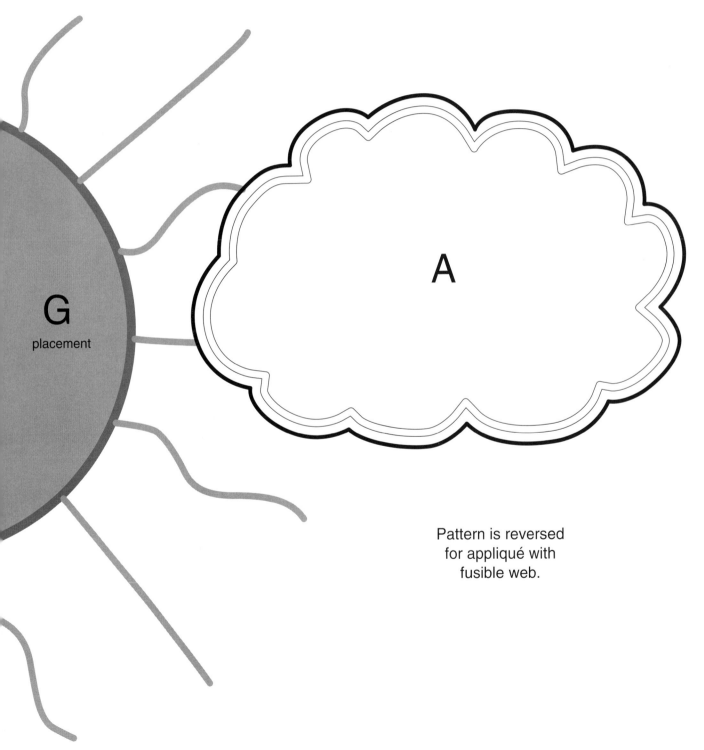

G
placement

A

Pattern is reversed
for appliqué with
fusible web.

Just Plane Fun Quilt

Chenille Color & Stitch Guide

02 Parsley ━━━━

MMMM Satin Stitch ━━━━

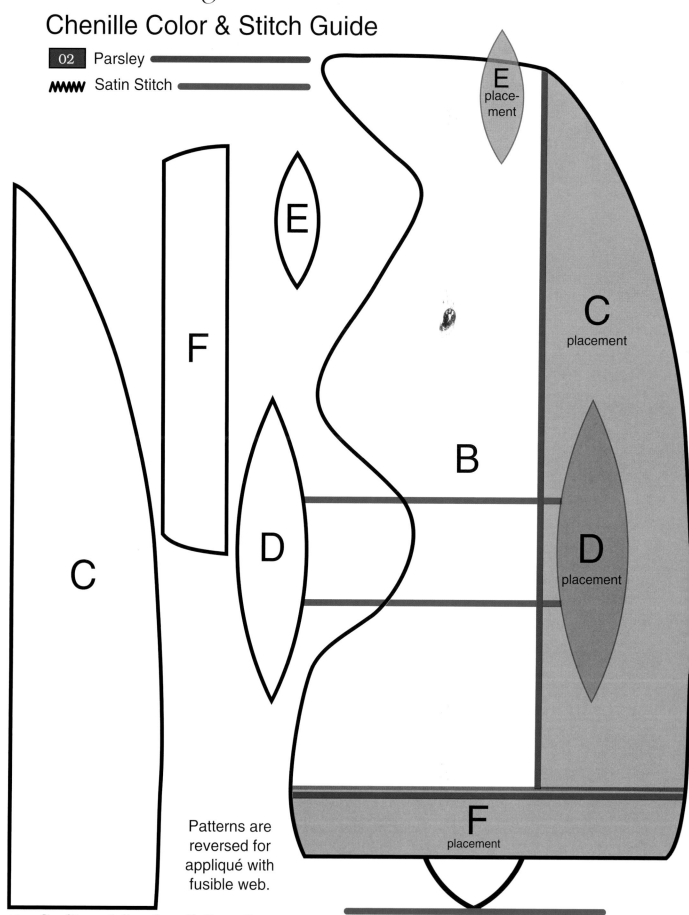

Patterns are reversed for appliqué with fusible web.

Just Plane Fun Quilt
Chenille Color Guide

08 | Banana

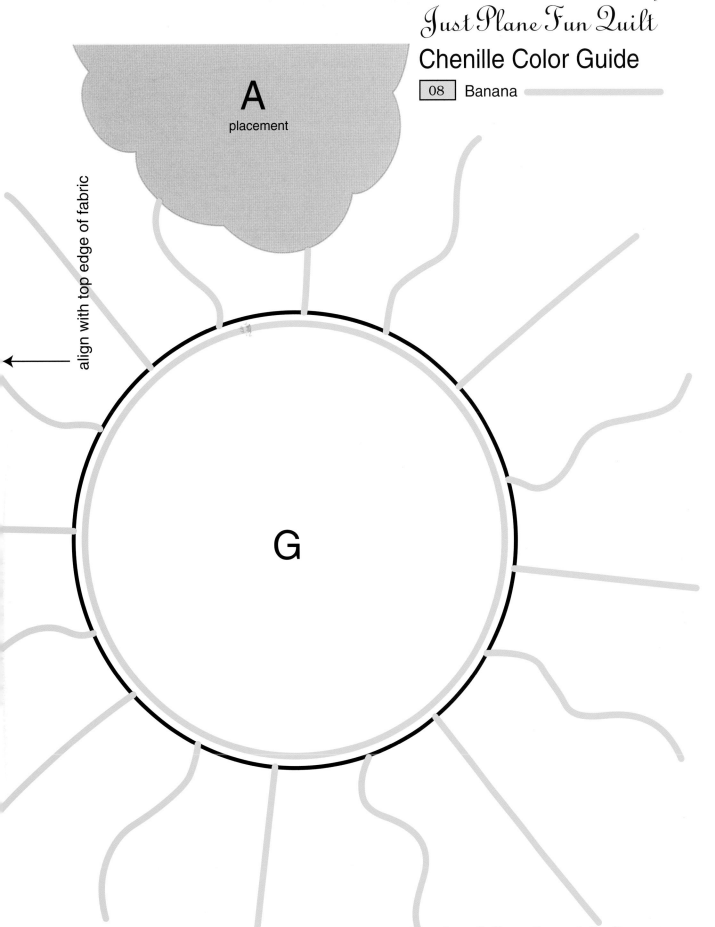

A
placement

align with top edge of fabric

G

Quilting Suggestion

The JUST PLANE FUN QUILT was quilted in the ditch. Then, the blue background blocks were quilted from side to side with a free-motion swirl pattern, leaving long horizontal quilted lines between swirls to create the idea of wind. The clouds were quilted with a free-motion mini-swirl pattern and the sun was stipple quilted.

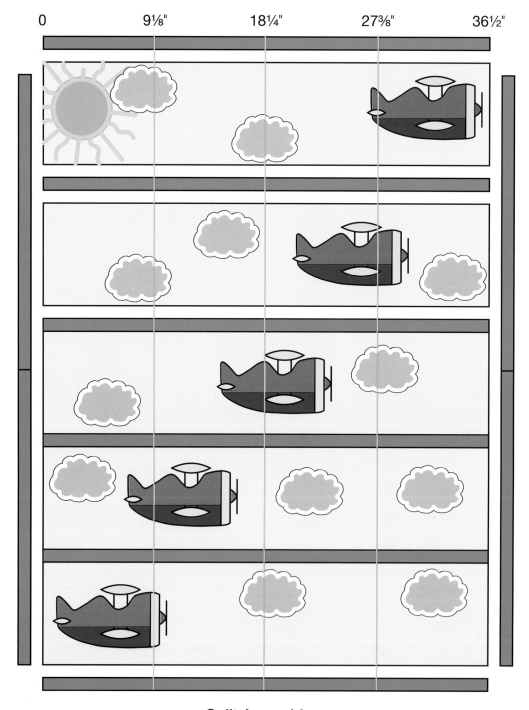

Quilt Assembly

Midnight Frolic Quilt

Finished size: 57" x 78¾"

Fabric and Cutting

WOF means width of fabric.
Yardage is based on a 40"–45" WOF.

Fabric	Yards	Cut	Dimension
Purple			
background panels	3⅞	6	12½" x WOF
binding		7	2¼" x WOF
block triangles		120	3½" squares, cut ◻
Yellow	½		
block triangles		6	6½" squares, cut ⊠
outer flower petals		3	A, page 41
Pink	½		
block triangles		6	6½" squares, cut ⊠
outer flower petals		3	A
Lime green	½		
block triangles		6	6½" squares, cut ⊠
outer flower petals		3	A
Orange	½		
block triangles		6	6½" squares, cut ⊠
outer flower petals		3	A
Blue	½		
block triangles			6½" squares, cut ⊠
outer flower petals		3	A
Multi-colored print	1¼		
inner flower petals		15	B, page 41
Backing	5	2	83" x WOF

Chenille By The Inch

Color		Amount
08	Banana	100"
20	Pumpkin	100"
10	Grape Soda	100"
06	Raspberry	100"
09	Blue Moon	100"
07	Limeade	325"

Additional Materials

Basic supplies as listed, pages 6 and 7
Purple sewing thread
Paper-backed fusible web
Yellow, pink, lime green, orange, and blue embroidery thread
Twin-sized (72" x 90") cotton batting
Monofilament quilting thread

① Referring to the block assembly guide, page 39, make 24 each of the yellow, pink, lime green, orange, and blue blocks. Sew the blocks together in two strips of 30 with a yellow, pink, green, orange, and blue color sequence. Sew two strips of 30 blocks with a pink, green, orange, blue, and yellow color sequence.

② Sew the purple background strips together in sets of two along the 12½" edge to make three panels. Following the quilt assembly guide, page 42, transfer A with a fabric marker to the center of one background panel, ¾" from the right edge. Transfer the vine placement line to each side of the flower as shown in the guide, page 40.

Transfer A to each end of the vine, ¾" from the left edge of the panel. Transfer the vine placement line to each of these flowers as shown. Transfer A to each end of the vine, ¾" from the right edge. There are five flowers and four vines for each panel. Repeat this process for the remaining panels.

3 Referring to Appliqué instructions, page 11, transfer A and B to the paper side of the fusible web and fuse them to the wrong side of the appropriate fabrics. Cut the patterns out on the drawn line.

Fuse one A of each color to the panels, referring to the quilt assembly guide for color placement and following the transferred lines. Fuse one B to each A. With lime green embroidery thread, appliqué the edges of B with a blanket stitch. Matching fabric and embroidery thread colors, appliqué the edges of A with a blanket stitch.

4 Referring to Chenille By The Inch instructions, page 8, remove the tear-away backing from the Banana, Pumpkin, Grape Soda, Raspberry, and Blue Moon chenille, but *do not cut chenille into strips*. Transfer three C patterns, page 41, to each color, centering the pattern edges between the pre-sewn lines. Cut the pattern out following the drawn line.

Pin one C to each flower, referring to the quilt photo, page 37, for color placement. Stitch the chenille on the pre-sewn lines, back tacking at the beginning and end to secure. With scissors, cut the chenille midway between the stitched lines, but *do not cut the background fabric*.

Remove the tear-away backing from the Limeade chenille, cut it into strips with a rotary cutter, and sew the strips around C and on the vines.

5 Center the background panels and trim them even with the block strips. Referring to the quilt assembly guide, page 42, piece the quilt top.

The chenille required for this project has been designed especially for the American Quilter's Society by Fabric Café®. See page 80.

6 Sew the backing pieces together along the 83" length and press the seam allowance open. Layer and baste the quilt top, batting, and backing. Machine quilt as desired (see suggestion, page 42). Sew the binding to the quilt, mitering corners. Fold the binding to the back, press, and hand stitch.

7 Referring to Chenille By The Inch instructions, page 9, use a spray bottle with distilled water to lightly mist the sewn chenille strips. Brush vigorously to fluff the chenille.

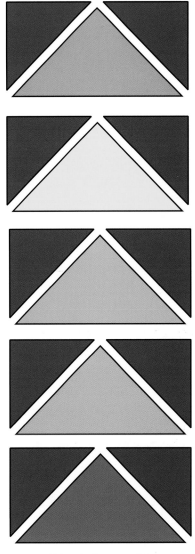

Block Assembly
Make 24 of each color

Midnight Frolic Quilt
Chenille Color Guide

| 07 | Limeade |——————————————

Chenille
Vine
Pattern

Placement
Guide

Midnight Frolic Quilt

Make three each of the following:
yellow, pink, lime green, orange, and blue

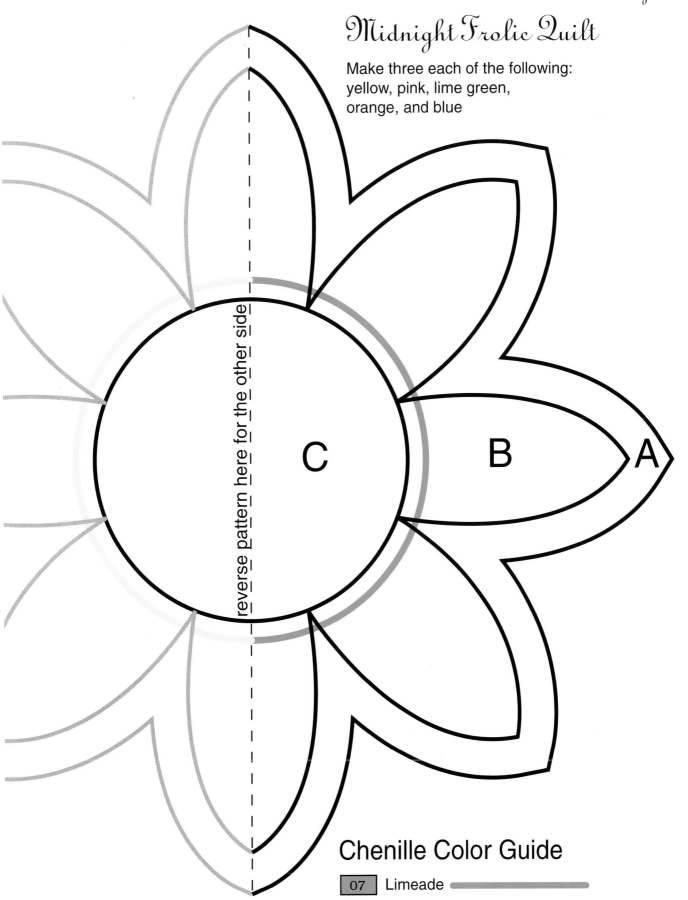

reverse pattern here for the other side

C

B

A

Chenille Color Guide

| 07 | Limeade |

Quilting Suggestion

The MIDNIGHT FROLIC QUILT was free-motion quilted in an allover swirl pattern.

Quilt Assembly

Primrose Path Quilt

Finished size: 60" x 60"

Fabric and Cutting

WOF means width of fabric. Yardage is based on a 40"–45" WOF. An "r" indicates that a pattern should be reversed.

Fabric	Yards	Cut	Dimension
White	3		
background blocks		9	8½" squares
border		4	6" squares
		8	6" x 24"
border blocks		8	3½" squares, cut ◻
side triangles		6	12⅝" squares, cut ⊠
corner triangles		2	6½" squares, cut ◻
Blue	1⅝		
border		16	1½" x WOF
binding		7	2¼" x WOF
joining blocks		64	1½" squares
border blocks		16	1" squares
flowers		13	A, page 46
Pink	⅝		
joining blocks		64	1½" x 6½"
border blocks		16	1" x 3¼"
Floral print	1		
joining blocks		16	6½" squares
border blocks		4	3¼" squares
flower centers		13	B, page 46
Green	⅞		
large leaves		9	C, page 46
small leaves		17	D, page 47
		8	Dr, page 47
Backing	3¾	2	64" x WOF

Chenille By The Inch

Color		Amount
02	Parsley	350"
03	Butterscotch	50"

Additional Materials

Basic supplies as listed, pages 6 and 7
Paper-backed fusible web
White sewing thread
Green, red, pink, and blue embroidery thread
Twin-sized (72" x 90") cotton batting
White quilting thread

1 Refer to the photo, page 43, for placement of the flower pattern, page 46, on the 8½" squares. With a fabric marker, transfer the pattern outlines and chenille placement lines to the blocks, placing the bottom point of the leaves ½" from the corner of the block.

Transfer the flower outlines and chenille lines, page 46, to the 6" border squares. Transfer the chenille lines, pages 46 and 47, and leaf outlines as indicated to four 6" x 24" border pieces. Reverse the pattern and transfer it to the remaining four pieces.

2 Referring to Appliqué instructions, page 11, transfer patterns A through Dr to the paper side of the fusible web and fuse them to the wrong side of the appropriate fabrics. Cut the patterns out on the drawn line and fuse them to the blocks, following the transferred placement lines. With a fabric marker, transfer the chenille and topstitch placement lines to the appliqué pieces.

3 With blue embroidery thread, appliqué the edges of A with a satin stitch. With red thread, appliqué the edges of B with a reverse blanket stitch. With green thread, appliqué the bottom edges of C, D, and Dr with a satin stitch, then appliqué the top edges with a reverse blanket stitch.

Following the topstitch lines on the patterns, topstitch B with pink thread and C, D, and Dr with green thread.

4 Referring to Chenille By The Inch instructions, page 8, prepare the chenille strips and sew them to the flower and border blocks.

5 Referring to the block assembly guides, page 48, piece 16 joining blocks with the 6½" floral squares, 1½" pink strips, and 1½" blue squares. Piece four border blocks with the 3¼" floral squares, 1" pink strips, 1" blue squares, and triangles cut from the 3½" white squares.

6 Referring to the quilt assembly guide, page 48, piece the center section of the quilt in diagonal strips of flower blocks, joining blocks, and side and corner triangles. Trim the side triangles even with the blocks. Sew the diagonal strips together.

Sew the ends of two 1½" blue strips together and press the seam allowance open. Repeat for the remaining blue strips. Sew the pieced strips to the top and bottom, then to the sides of the quilt top. Press and trim each strip to size.

7 Sew a border block between two 6" x 24" border pieces. Repeat to make four pieced borders. Sew two borders to the sides of the quilt top. Sew a corner block to each end of the remaining pieced borders, then sew one to the top and bottom of the quilt top.

Sew two pieced 1½" blue strips to the top and bottom, then two strips to the sides of the quilt top. Press and trim each strip to size.

8 Sew the backing pieces together along the 64" length and press the seam allowance open. Layer and baste the quilt top, batting, and backing. Machine quilt as desired (see suggestion, page 48). Sew the binding to the quilt, mitering corners. Fold the binding to the back, press, and hand stitch.

9 Referring to Chenille By The Inch instructions, page 9, use a spray bottle with distilled water to lightly mist the sewn chenille strips. Brush vigorously to fluff the chenille.

Primrose Path Quilt

Flower Pattern

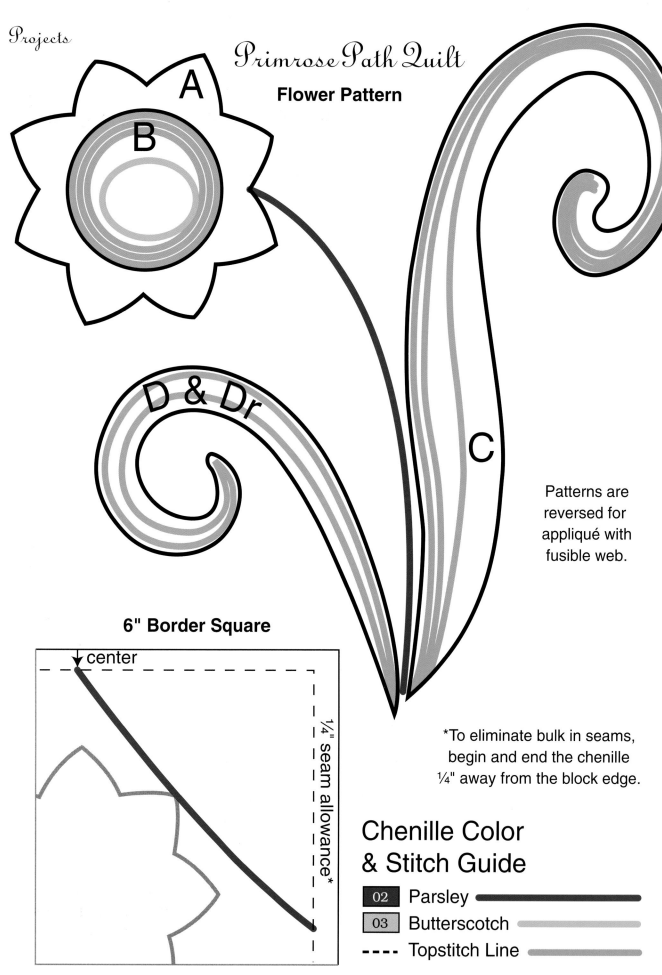

A

B

D & Dr

C

Patterns are reversed for appliqué with fusible web.

6" Border Square

center

¼" seam allowance*

*To eliminate bulk in seams, begin and end the chenille ¼" away from the block edge.

Chenille Color & Stitch Guide

02	Parsley
03	Butterscotch
- - -	Topstitch Line

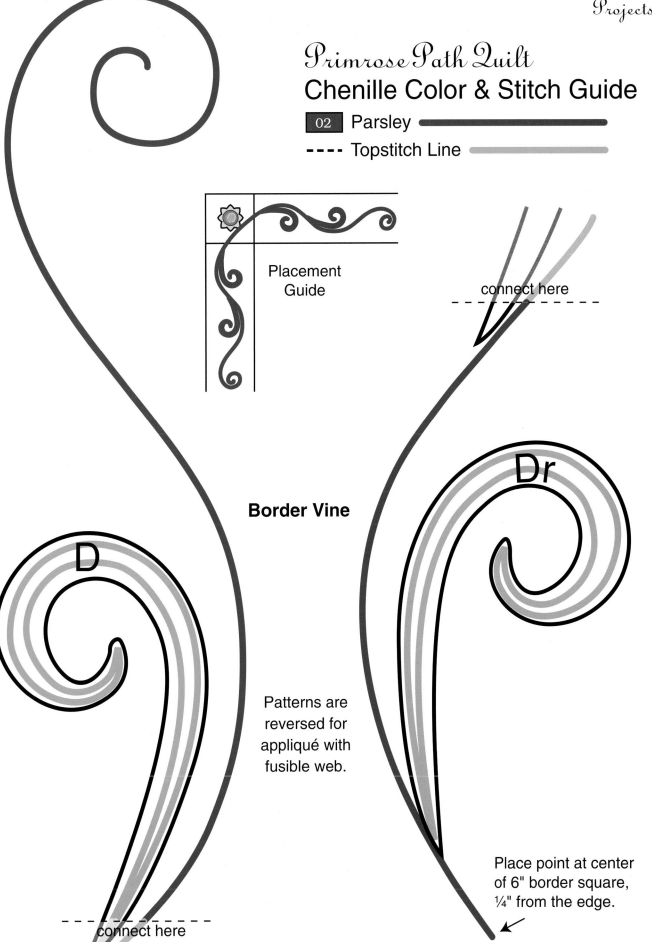

Primrose Path Quilt
Chenille Color & Stitch Guide

02	Parsley
- - - -	Topstitch Line

Placement Guide

connect here

Border Vine

Dr

D

Patterns are reversed for appliqué with fusible web.

connect here

Place point at center of 6" border square, ¼" from the edge.

Joining Block Assembly

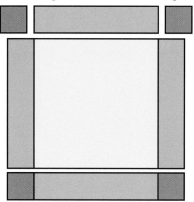

Border Block Assembly

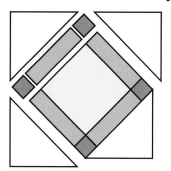

Quilting Suggestion

The PRIMROSE PATH QUILT was entirely free-motion quilted, starting with quilting in the ditch, then adding an 8" daisy design on the pieced blocks. The same daisy was used on the setting triangles, but was halved and quartered to fit. All appliqué was echo quilted, then a ½" grid was added behind the flowers, along with a 1" diagonal line behind the border vines.

Quilt Assembly

Reminiscence Baby Quilt

Finished size: 38" x 38"

Fabric and Cutting

WOF means width of fabric.
Yardage is based on a 40"–45" WOF.

Fabric	Yards	Cut	Dimension
Yellow	⅔		
blocks		13	6½" squares
Purple	1¼		
border		4	4½" x WOF
binding		5	2¼" x WOF
blocks		12	3½" squares ⊠
Blue	¼	12	4¼" squares, cut ◩
Pink	½	24	3⅞" squares, cut
Backing	1½	1	42" square

Additional Materials
Basic supplies as listed, pages 6 and 7
White sewing thread
Crib-sized (45" x 60") cotton batting
Yellow quilting thread

Chenille By The Inch

Color		Amount
25	Jelly Bean	130"
10	Grape Soda	120"
21	Cotton Candy	50"
06	Raspberry	20"
24	Gum Drop	130"
04	Blueberry	100"
08	Banana	425"

1 Referring to the block assembly guide, page 51, piece the block with one purple square, four blue triangles, and four pink triangles. Make 12 pieced blocks.

2 Fold a yellow block in half, then in half again, and finger press to mark the center. With a fabric marker, transfer the chenille placement lines, page 52, to the center of the yellow block.

3 Referring to Chenille By The Inch instructions, page 8, prepare the chenille strips and sew them to the block. To make the center dots in the flowers, cut a ⅜" piece of chenille and sew it to the placement line. Make seven blocks with purple flowers and six blocks with blue flowers.

4 Referring to the quilt assembly guide, page 54, alternate the blocks and sew them together in five strips of five. Sew the strips together. Sew the 4½" purple border strips to the top and bottom, then to the sides of the quilt top. Press and trim each strip to size.

5 With a fabric marker, transfer the chenille placement lines, page 53, to the border. Placing the pattern 1" from the inside seam and centering three loops over each block, repeat the pattern to the corner. Sew the chenille strips to the border, following the transferred placement lines.

6 Layer and baste the quilt top, batting, and backing. Machine quilt as desired (see suggestion, page 54). Sew the binding to the quilt, mitering the corners. Fold the binding to the back, press, and hand stitch.

7 Referring to Chenille By The Inch instructions, page 9, use a spray bottle with distilled water to lightly mist the sewn chenille strips. Brush vigorously to fluff the chenille.

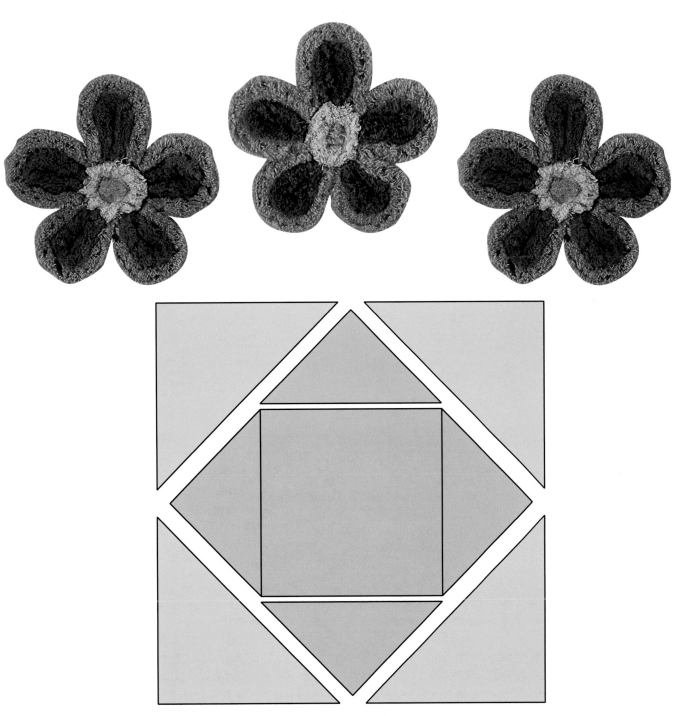

Block Assembly

Reminiscence Baby Quilt
Purple Flower Color Guide

Make 7

25	Jelly Bean	
10	Grape Soda	
21	Cotton Candy	
06	Raspberry	

Purple Flower

Quilting Pattern

Blue Flower Color Guide

Make 6

24	Gum Drop	
04	Blueberry	
21	Cotton Candy	
06	Raspberry	

Blue Flower

Reminiscence Baby Quilt

Border Pattern

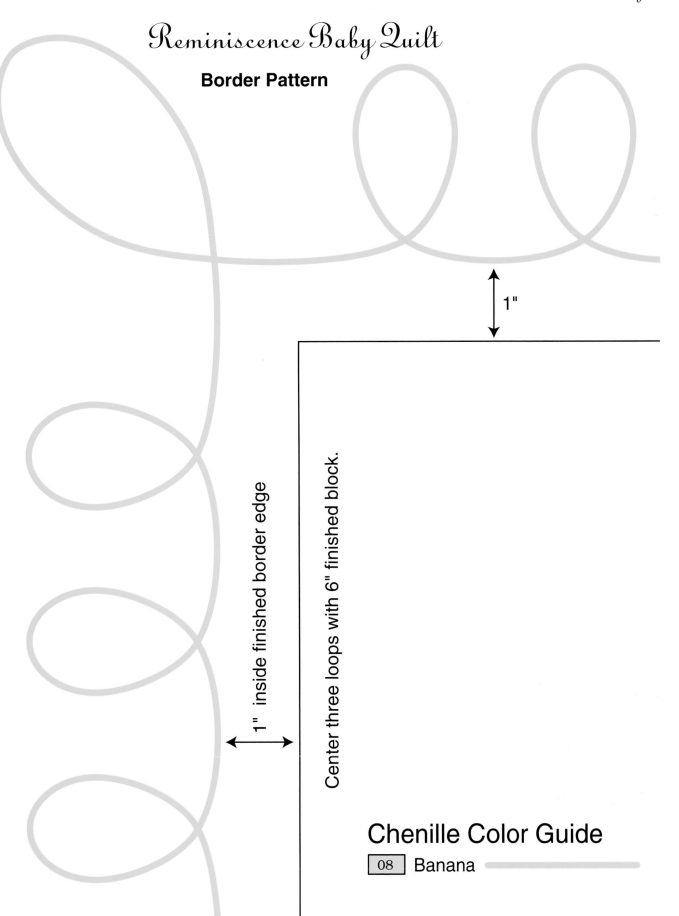

1"

1" inside finished border edge

Center three loops with 6" finished block.

Chenille Color Guide

| 08 | Banana |

Quilting Suggestion

The REMINISCENCE BABY QUILT was quilted in the ditch and free-motion echo quilted around the chenille flowers and border. The flower design, page 52, was quilted in the center of the pieced blocks.

Quilt Assembly

Caribbean Garden Wallhanging

Finished size: 23" x 23"

Fabric and Cutting

WOF means width of fabric. Yardage is based on a 40"–45" WOF. An "r" indicates that a pattern should be reversed.

Fabric	Yards	Cut	Dimension
Pink	½		
binding		3	2¼" x WOF
flowers		4	A, page 57
White	⅓		
blocks		4	6½" squares
border		16	3½" x 1½"
Gold	½		
sashing		6	6½" x 3½"
		3	21½" x 3½"
Lime green	⅓		
vines		2	B, page 58
		1	Br, page 58
Purple	¼		
border		12	3½" x 1½"
		4	1½" squares
Backing	1	1	27" square

Chenille By The Inch

Color		Amount
07	Limeade	10"
10	Grape Soda	100"

Additional Materials
Basic supplies as listed, pages 6 and 7
Paper-backed fusible web
White sewing thread
Green and pink embroidery thread
Gold metallic ⅛" ribbon
Crib-sized (45" x 60") cotton batting
Monofilament quilting thread

1 Referring to Appliqué instructions, page 11, transfer A, B, and Br to the paper side of the fusible web and fuse to the wrong side of the appropriate fabrics. Cut the patterns out on the drawn line. With a fabric marker, draw the chenille and metallic ribbon placement lines on the A pieces.

2 Fuse the flower to the center of the 6½" white blocks. Fuse the vines to center bottom edge of the 21½" gold sashing. With pink embroidery thread, appliqué the edges of the flowers with a blanket stitch. With green embroidery thread, appliqué the inside edges of the vines.

3 Following the placement lines on A, couch metallic ribbon to the flowers, using small stitches at regular intervals. Couch metallic ribbon to the outside edges of the vines.

4 Referring to the quilt assembly guide, page 59, piece the flower blocks and sashing in five vertical strips. Sew the strips together.

5 To make a border strip, sew four white and three 3½" x 1½" purple rectangles together, end to end. Make four borders. Sew one border to the each side of the wallhanging. Sew a 1½" purple square to each end of the remaining two border strips, then sew the strips to the top and bottom of the wallhanging.

6 Referring to Chenille By The Inch instructions, page 8, prepare the chenille strips for sewing. To make the center dots in the flowers, cut a ⅜" piece from the Limeade chenille strip and sew it to the placement lines. Sew Grape Soda chenille to the seams around the flower blocks.

7 Layer and baste the wallhanging top, batting, and backing. Machine quilt as desired (see suggestion, page 59). Sew the binding to the wallhanging, mitering corners. Fold the binding to the back, press, and hand stitch.

8 Referring to Chenille By The Inch instructions, page 9, use a spray bottle with distilled water to lightly mist the sewn chenille strips. Brush vigorously to fluff the chenille.

Caribbean Garden Wallhanging
Chenille Color & Embellishment Guide

| 07 | Limeade
Metallic Ribbon

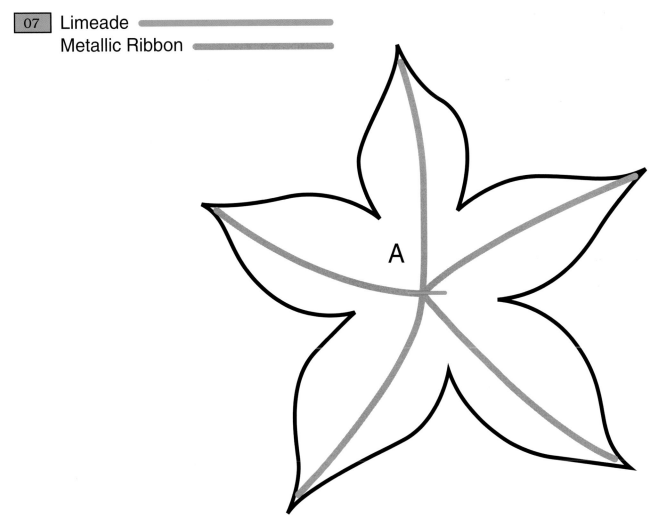

A

Caribbean Garden Wallhanging

Vine Pattern

connect here

Pattern is reversed for appliqué with fusible web.

B & Br

B & Br

connect here

stop here for center vine

B

Br

Br

Placement Guide

Quilting Suggestion

The flower blocks of the CARIBBEAN GARDEN WALLHANGING were stipple quilted. The sashing was quilted with a free-motion pattern mimicking the vine pattern.

Quilt Assembly

Little Lamb Wallhanging

Finished size: 22½" x 22½"

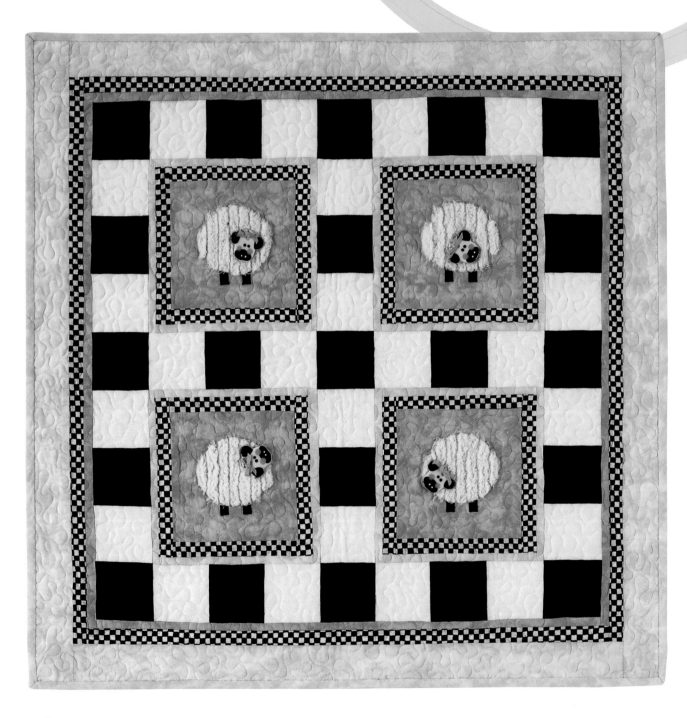

Fabric and Cutting

WOF means width of fabric.
Yardage is based on a 40"–45" WOF.

Fabric	Yards	Cut	Dimension
Purple	¼		
border		2	¾" x WOF
blocks		4	5" squares
Pink	⅔		
block border		3	¾" x WOF
border		4	2" x WOF
binding		3	2¼" x WOF
Black-and-white check	¼		
block border		3	1" x WOF
border		4	1" x WOF
Black	¼		
sashing		21	2½" squares
lamb legs		8	A, page 62
White	¼		
sashing		24	2½" squares
Backing	1	1	27" x 27"

Chenille By The Inch

Color		Amount
12	Coconut	200"

Additional Materials

Additional Materials
Basic supplies as listed, pages 6 and 7
Paper-backed fusible web
Black embroidery thread
White sewing thread
Crib-sized (45" x 60") cotton batting
Monofilament quilting thread
Four 1" porcelain lamb face buttons
½ yard ⅛" wide pink satin ribbon

1 With a fabric marker, transfer A and B outlines to the center of the 5" purple block. Referring to Appliqué instructions, page 11, transfer A to the paper side of the fusible web and fuse it to the wrong side of the black fabric. Cut the pattern out on the drawn line. Fuse A to the blocks. With black embroidery thread, appliqué the edges of A with a satin stitch.

2 Referring to Chenille By The Inch instructions, page 8, remove the tear-away backing from the chenille, but *do not cut chenille into strips.* Transfer B to one side of the chenille, centering the pattern edges between the pre-sewn lines. Cut the pattern out and pin it to the block. Stitch the chenille on the pre-sewn lines, back tacking at the beginning and end to secure. With scissors, cut the chenille midway between the stitched lines, but do not cut the background fabric.

3 To complete the lamb block, sew a 1" black-and-white checked strip to the top and bottom, then to the sides of the block. Press and trim each strip to size. Sew a ¾" pink strip to the block in the same manner. Make four bordered blocks.

4 For the sashing, refer to the quilt assembly guide and sew five black and four white 2½" squares together alternately. Make three strips. Sew one black and two white 2½" squares together alternately. Make six strips.

5 Referring to the quilt assembly guide, page 63, piece the center section of the wallhanging in five strips of blocks and sashing strips. Sew the strips together.

6 Cut the two ¾" purple strips in half. Sew a strip to the top and bottom, then to the sides of the wallhanging. Press and trim each strip to size. Sew the 1" black-and-white checked strips and the 2" pink strips to the wallhanging in the same manner.

7 Layer and baste the wallhanging top, batting, and backing. Machine quilt as desired (see suggestion, page 63). Sew the binding to the wallhanging, mitering corners. Fold the binding to the back, press, and hand stitch.

8 Referring to Chenille By The Inch instructions, page 9, use a spray bottle with distilled water to lightly mist the sewn chenille strips. Brush vigorously to fluff the chenille.

9 Randomly place porcelain lamb face buttons on the lamb bodies and sew. Thread pink satin ribbon through the button holes on the lamb faces, tie a bow, and trim the ends. *Note: Quilts with buttons should not be given to children under the age of five.*

Little Lamb Wallhanging
Chenille Color Guide

| 12 | Coconut ⬭ |

B

A

A placement

Pattern B is transferred
to the Coconut chenille.
See step 2, page 61.

Quilting Suggestion

The LITTLE LAMB WALLHANGING was free-motion stipple quilted.

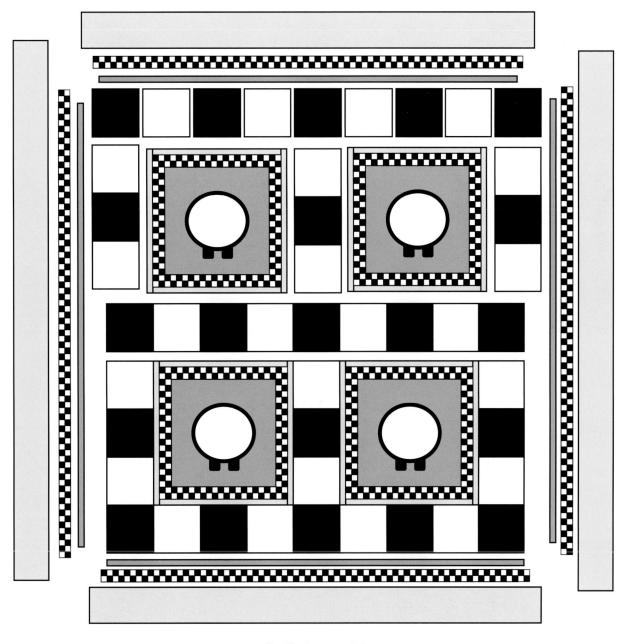

Quilt Assembly

Starlight Wallhanging

Finished size: 23" x 23"

Fabric and Cutting

WOF means width of fabric.
Yardage is based on a 40"–45" WOF.

Fabric	Yards	Cut	Dimension
Dark blue	1		
strips		7	1½" x WOF
border		4	2" x WOF
binding		3	2¼" x WOF
Royal blue	⅓		
strips		7	1½" x WOF
Purple	⅓		
strips		7	1½" x WOF
Light purple	⅓		
strips		7	1½" x WOF
Backing	1	1	27" x WOF

Chenille By The Inch

Color		Amount
10	Grape Soda	35"
25	Jelly Bean	45"

Additional Materials
Basic supplies as listed, pages 6 and 7
Blue sewing thread
Silver metallic braid #16 weight
Silver 3 mm beads
Purple 3 mm bugle beads
Silver 9 mm bugle beads
Crib-sized (45" x 60") cotton batting
Purple quilting thread

1 Sew one each dark blue, royal blue, purple, and light purple 1½" strips together as shown in the block assembly guide, page 66. Make seven of these strip-sets. Following the lines shown, cut 3" squares at a 45-degree angle from the strip-sets to make 64 blocks.

2 Referring to the quilt assembly guide, piece the center of the wallhanging top in eight strips of eight blocks, alternating the direction of the blocks. Sew the strips together.

3 Referring to Chenille By The Inch instructions, page 8, prepare the chenille strips for sewing. Following the embellishment guide, sew the chenille and metallic braid to the wallhanging.

4 Sew a 2" dark blue strip to the top and bottom, then to the sides of the wallhanging. Press and trim each strip to size.

5 Layer and baste the wallhanging top, batting, and backing. Machine quilt as desired (see suggestion, page 67). Sew the binding to the wallhanging, mitering corners. Fold the binding to the back, press, and hand stitch.

6 Referring to Chenille By The Inch instructions, page 9, use a spray bottle with distilled water to lightly mist the sewn chenille strips. Brush vigorously to fluff the chenille.

7 Sew the beads to the wallhanging as shown in the embellishment guide, page 66.

Starlight Wallhanging

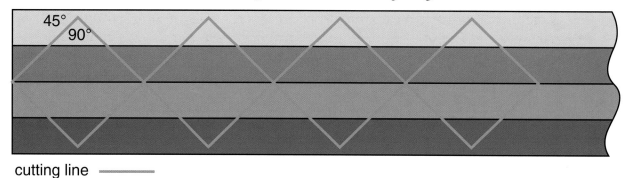

45°
90°

cutting line ——————

Block Assembly

Chenille Color & Embellishment Guide

| 10 | Grape Soda ———————— |
| 25 | Jelly Bean ———————— |

Jelly Bean (#25) is actually blue.
We used green in the guide so you could see it better.

Silver 3 mm beads ● ● ● ● ● ● ● ● ●
Purple 3 mm bugle beads - - - - - - - -
Silver 9 mm bugle beads — — — — —
Metallic braid ————————

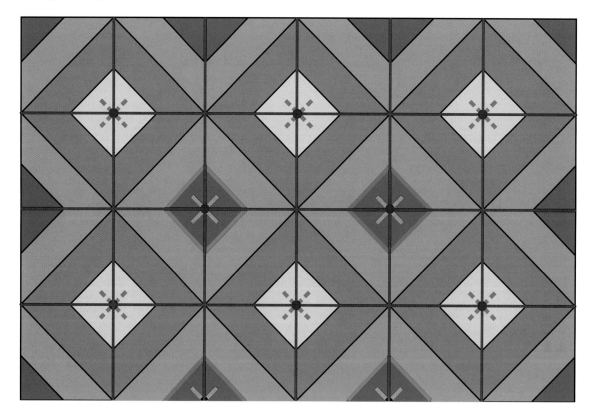

Quilting Suggestion

The STARLIGHT WALLHANGING was quilted in the ditch along the purple and royal blue seam lines. The quilting along the royal blue seam lines was continued into the border to give the illusion of an extended block.

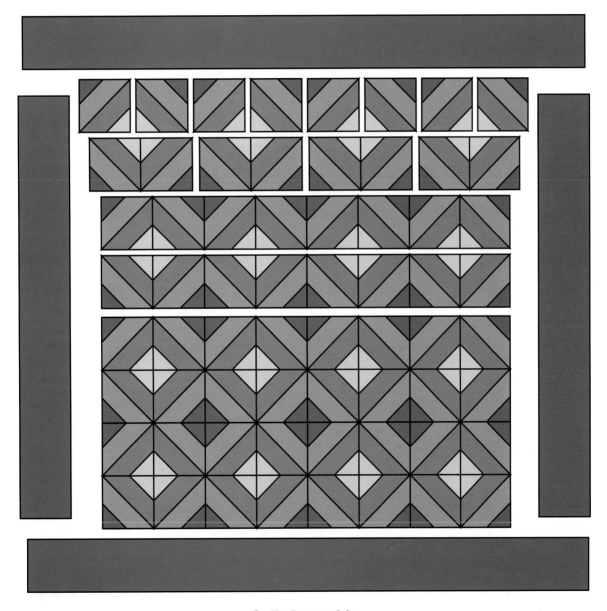

Quilt Assembly

Dancing Redwork Table Runner

Finished size: 18" x 48"

Fabric and Cutting

Cut borders first, parallel to the selvage.
WOF means width of fabric.
Yardage is based on a 40"–45" WOF.

Fabric	Yards	Cut	Dimension
White	1¼		
border		2	3½" x 42½"
		2	3½" x 12½"
blocks		28	3½" squares
appliqué		32	A, page 70
Red*	1		
border		4	2¼" x WOF
blocks		32	3½" squares
appliqué		28	A
Backing	1⅔	1	22" x 52"
*Three assorted prints to total 1 yard			

Chenille By The Inch

Color		Amount
01	Strawberry	230"

Additional Materials
Basic supplies as listed, pages 6 and 7
Paper-backed fusible web
White sewing thread
Red and white embroidery thread
Crib-sized (45" x 60") cotton batting
Monofilament quilting thread

1 Referring to Appliqué instructions, page 11, transfer A to the paper side of the fusible web and fuse it to the wrong side of the appropriate fabrics. Cut the pattern out on the drawn line. Fuse the white A pieces to the 3½" assorted red blocks, and the assorted red A pieces to the 3½" white blocks. Matching embroidery thread with the A pieces, appliqué the edges with a blanket stitch.

2 Referring to the quilt assembly guide, page 71, sew the blocks together, alternating red and white blocks in four strips of 14 blocks. Sew the strips together.

3 Draw a line with a fabric marker through the center length of the 12½" and 42½" white border strips. Sew a border strip to each long side of the table runner and press. Sew a red block to each end of the 12½" border strips, then sew these strips to each short side of the runner and press.

4 With a fabric marker, transfer the chenille placement lines, page 70, to the borders of the table runner, centering the design. Repeat the pattern to each corner block.

5 Referring to Chenille By The Inch instructions, page 8, prepare the chenille strips and sew them to the border.

6 Layer and baste the table runner top, batting, and backing. Machine quilt as desired (see suggestion, page 71). Sew the binding to the table runner, mitering corners. Fold the binding to the back, press, and hand stitch.

7 Referring to Chenille By The Inch instructions, page 9, use a spray bottle with distilled water to lightly mist the sewn chenille strips. Brush vigorously to fluff the chenille.

Dancing Redwork Table Runner

Chenille Color Guide

01 Strawberry

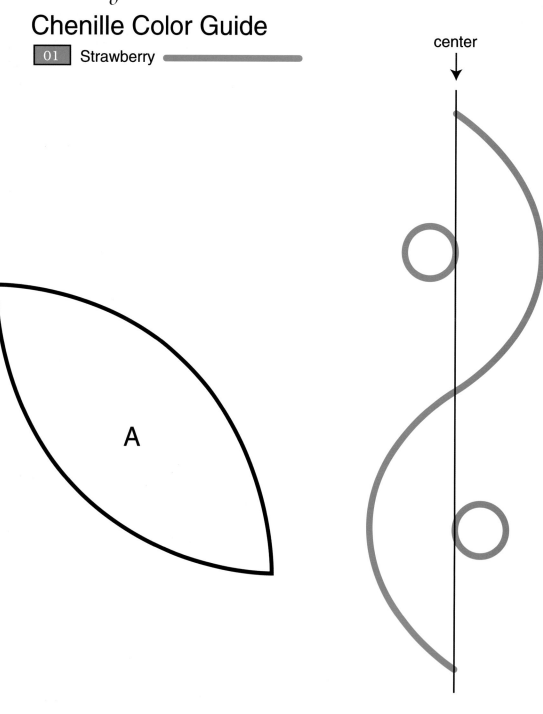

center

A

Border Pattern

Quilting Suggestion

The DANCING REDWORK TABLE RUNNER was quilted in the ditch and on each side of the appliqué pieces. The chenille design on the border was echo quilted.

Quilt Assembly

Vineyard Romance Table Runner

Finished size: 21½" x 50¼"

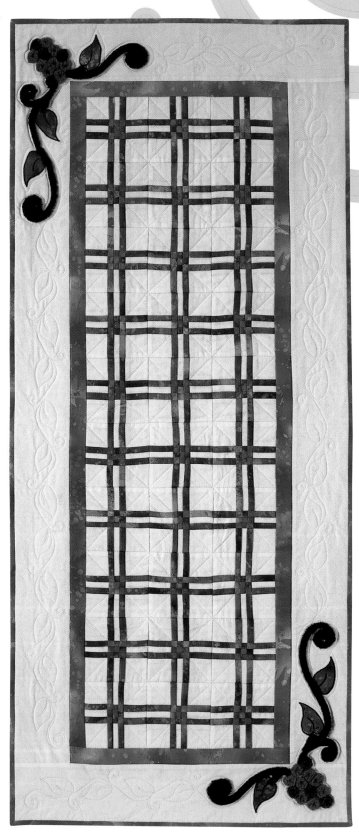

Fabric and Cutting

Cut borders first, parallel to the selvage.
WOF means width of fabric.
RW means remaining width.
Yardage is based on a 40"–45" WOF.

Fabric	Yards	Cut	Dimension
White	2		
border		3	4" x 46"
strips		10	2" x RW
		4	⅞" x RW
Green	¾		
strips		12	⅞" x WOF
		4	2" x WOF
leaves		6	A, page 76
Purple	1⅔		
border		3	1½" x 44"
strips		5	⅞" x RW
binding		4	2¼" x RW
Backing	1⅔	1	26" x 55"

Chenille By The Inch

	Color	Amount
05	Eggplant	20"
10	Grape Soda	40"
17	Basil	60"

Additional Materials
Basic supplies as listed, pages 6 and 7
White sewing thread
Paper-backed fusible web
Green embroidery thread
Crib-sized (45" x 60") cotton batting
White quilting thread

1 Referring to the strip-set assembly guides, page 75, piece Strip-Set 1 with the following strips: two 2" white, two ⅞" green, and one ⅞" white. Make four sets, press, and cut into sixty 2" segments.

Piece Strip-Set 2 with the following strips: two 2" green, two ⅞" purple, and one ⅞" green. Make two sets, press, and cut into sixty ⅞" segments.

Piece Strip-Set 3 with the following strips: two 2" white, two ⅞" green, and one ⅞" purple. Make one set, press, and cut into thirty ⅞" segments.

2 Piece the strip-set segments into 30 blocks, following the block assembly guide, page 75. Referring to the quilt assembly guide, page 78, sew the blocks together in three strips of 10 blocks. Sew the strips together.

3 Sew a 1½" purple strip to each long side of the table runner. Press and trim the strips to size. Cut the remaining 1½" purple strip in half and sew a half to each short side of the table runner. Press and trim the strips to size. Sew the 4" white border strips to the table runner in the same manner.

4 Refer to the photo, page 72, for placement of the grapevine pattern, page 76, on the borders. With a fabric marker, transfer the pattern and chenille placement lines to two corners of the table runner.

5 Transfer A to the paper side of the fusible web following Appliqué instructions, page 11, and fuse it to the wrong side of the appropriate fabric. Cut the pattern out on the drawn line. Fuse A to the border. With green embroidery thread, appliqué the leaf edges and vein lines with a satin stitch.

6 Referring to Chenille By The Inch instructions, page 8, prepare the chenille strips and sew to the border.

7 Layer and baste the table runner top, batting, and backing. Machine quilt as desired (see suggestion, page 78). Sew the binding to the table runner, mitering corners. Fold the binding to the back, press, and hand stitch.

8 Referring to Chenille By The Inch instructions, page 9, use a spray bottle with distilled water to lightly mist the sewn chenille strips. Brush vigorously to fluff the chenille.

Vineyard Romance Table Runner

Strip-Set 1

Cut into sixty 2" segments.

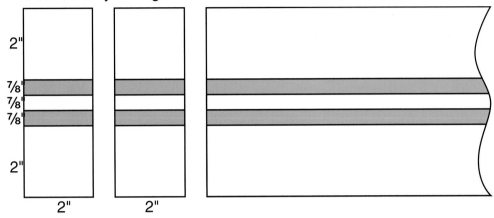

Strip-Set 2

Cut into sixty ⅞" segments.

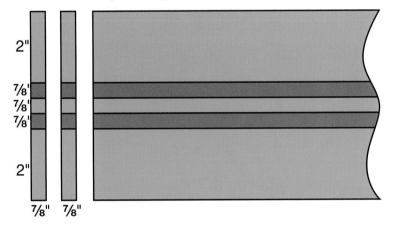

Strip-Set 3

Cut into thirty ⅞" segments.

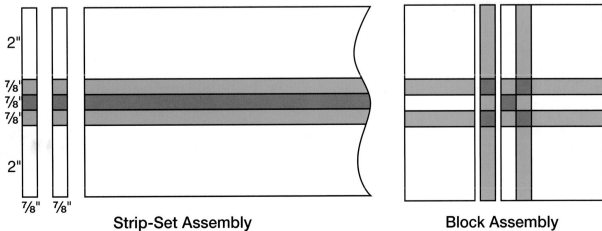

Strip-Set Assembly   **Block Assembly**

Vineyard Romance Table Runner
Chenille Color & Stitch Guide

05	Eggplant	
10	Grape Soda	
17	Basil	
MWMW	Satin Stitch	

Pattern Guide

Grapevine Pattern

Reverse A
for appliqué
with fusible web.

A

A

connect here

A

connect here

Vineyard Romance Table Runner

Continuous-Line
Quilting Pattern

finish

start

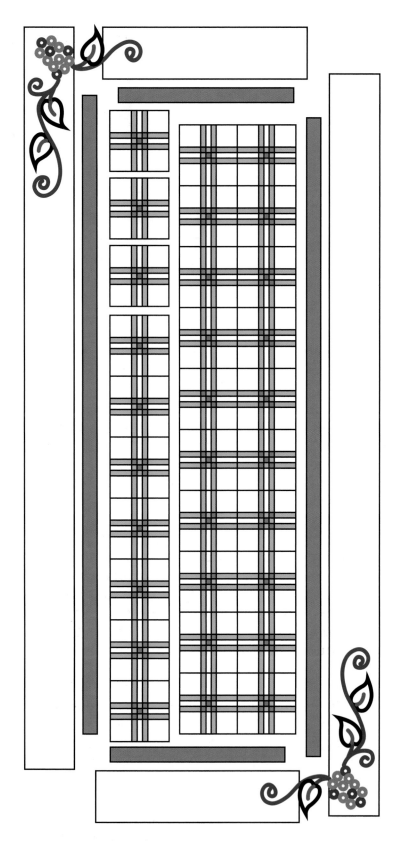

Quilt Assembly

Quilting Suggestion

The Vineyard Romance Table Runner was entirely free-motion quilted. It was quilted in the ditch first, then diagonally from corner to corner of the blocks. The continuous-line leaf pattern, page 77, was quilted on the white borders.

About the Author

At the early age of six, Fran Morgan began sewing and exploring needlework. By the time she was a teenager, she had mastered many needlecraft techniques, including sewing, needle-point, crochet, cross-stitch, and knitting. As a result of this early exposure, Fran developed extensive knowledge, experience, and a genuine love for needlecraft and sewing.

In pursuit of her passion, Fran went to work for The Needlecraft Shop, Ltd. at the age of 18. Not only did this publishing division provide the opportunity to further expand Fran's sewing skills, it cultivated a professional presence for her in the industry. She designed over 50 needlecraft project books, and in time, became responsible for the design acquisition department.

In 2000, Fran also became the developing editor for *Sewing Savvy* magazine. After 14 years with The Needlecraft Shop, Fran decided to seek other opportunities. In her home studio, Fran began experimenting with faux chenille techniques. After many months, she discovered an easy method for replicating the look and feel of old-fashioned chenille. After sharing the innovation with her mother, the two became business partners and co-founded Fabric Café® in January 2001. Together, they created and marketed their first product, Chenille By The Inch™.

Since then, Fran has realized many of her ambitions while creating and publishing original quilt designs for Fabric Café. In addition to publishing over 25 designs under the Fabric Café logo, her designs have been featured on the covers of magazines such as *Sew News*, *McCall's Quick Quilts*, and *The Quilter Magazine*. She has appeared as a guest on television shows such as *America Sews*, *Quilting with Shar*, *Sew Much More*, and *Simply Quilts*.

Fran shares her enthusiasm for sewing and Chenille By The Inch through presentations and classes at trade and consumer shows. She has been a member of the Society of Craft Designers since 1986 and currently serves on the board of directors.

Other AQS Books & Products

This is only a small selection of the books and products available from the American Quilter's Society. AQS books are known worldwide for timely topics, clear writing, beautiful color photos, and accurate illustrations and patterns. The following items are available from your local bookseller or quilt shop.

#6511   us$22.95

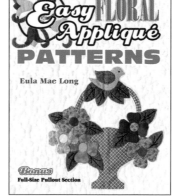

#6300   us$24.95

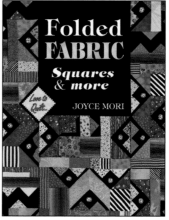

#6207   us$16.95

Great Buy!

Select one of these handy project packs and get enough Chenille By The Inch™ to complete your chosen project. It's a quick, easy way to get started on your next quilt.

pg. 17

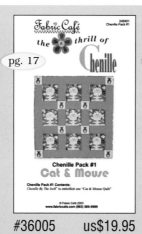

#36005   us$19.95

pg. 30

#36006   us$19.95

pg. 37

#36004   us$39.95

Strawberry ①	Parsley ②	Butterscotch ③	Blueberry ④	Eggplant ⑤
Raspberry ⑥	Limeade ⑦	Banana ⑧	Blue Moon ⑨	Grape Soda ⑩
Almond ⑪	Coconut ⑫	Cappuccino ⑬	Licorice ⑭	Chocolate ⑮
Wine ⑯	Basil ⑰	Spice ⑱	Boysenberry ⑲	Pumpkin ⑳
Cotton Candy ㉑	Key Lime Pie ㉒	Lemon Ice ㉓	Gum Drop ㉔	Jelly Bean ㉕

The Secret to Fluffy Chenille

Chenille Brush™
with Cutting Guide
#33012 . . . us$10.95

Get perfect fabric strips with every cut.
Take the strips from flat to fluffy in a jiffy.

Chenille By The Inch™ Packs

Single color, 100 inch packages come in 25 delicious colors, by Fabric Café™. Available at your local quilt shops. Retail $5 each.

LOOK for these items nationally. **CALL** **1-800-626-5420**
or **VISIT** our Web site at **www.AQSquilt.com**